What Does a
MAYOR Do?

David J. Jakubiak

PowerKiDS press™

New York

To Robert Hill, who loves The City

Published in 2010 by The Rosen Publishing Group, Inc.
29 East 21st Street, New York, NY 10010

First Edition

Editor: Amelie von Zumbusch
Book Design: Julio Gil
Photo Researcher: Jessica Gerweck

Photo Credits: Cover Spencer Platt/Getty Images; p. 5 Joe Murphy/NBAE via Getty Images; p. 6 Shutterstock.com; p. 9 Mario Tama/Getty Images; p. 10 Paul J. Richards/AFP/Getty Images; p. 13 John Kelly/Getty Images; p. 14 Mark Ralston/AFP/Getty Images; p. 17 Bill Pugliano/Getty Images; p. 18 Mike Coppola/FilmMagic/Getty Images; p. 21 George Rose/Getty Images.

Library of Congress Cataloging-in-Publication Data

Jakubiak, David J.
  What does a mayor do? / David J. Jakubiak.
    p. cm. — (How our government works)
  Includes index.
  ISBN 978-1-4358-9359-7 (library binding) — ISBN 978-1-4358-9814-1 (pbk.) — ISBN 978-1-4358-9815-8 (6-pack)
  1. Mayors—Juvenile literature. I. Title.
  JS141.J35 2010
  352.23'216—dc22

                          2009030405

Manufactured in the United States of America

CPSIA Compliance Information: Batch #WW10PK: For Further Information contact Rosen Publishing, New York, New York at 1-800-237-9932

CONTENTS

TIME TO MEET THE MAYOR

Two **tornadoes** rolled through Springfield, Illinois, in March 2006. Homes were destroyed. Businesses were torn apart. There was no power. Damage seemed to be everywhere. Springfield mayor Timothy J. Davlin called on the people of his city and the surrounding towns to help. Thousands of people came to the city to work. A week later, power was back, the streets were clear, and life was almost back to normal.

The United States is led by the president. Every state has a governor. Cities and towns have leaders, too. In many communities, those people are called mayors.

Here, Boston, Massachusetts, mayor Thomas Menino cuts a ribbon at the opening of a reading and learning center at the city's Blackstone Community Center.

Local governments are often in charge of keeping streets clear of snow and ice during the winter. Many towns and cities have their own snowplows, like the one shown here.

YOUR LOCAL GOVERNMENT

When a new firehouse opened in Louisville, Kentucky, in 2009, Mayor Jerry Abramson proudly stood with the fire chief. The new station took the place of one that was over 100 years old.

Local governments may have an official building, often known as a city hall or municipal center. Here, mayors can meet with other leaders or with people who live in their communities.

Every level of government has important jobs. For example, the national government keeps the country safe. State governments run state parks. Local governments may be in charge of fire departments, libraries, schools, and trash collection. Some jobs are shared by all levels of government. Local governments build some roads, while state governments and the national government build others.

PICKING A LOCAL LEADER

In 2001, Michael Bloomberg won an election to become the mayor of New York City. The election was closely watched because it was held two months after **terrorists** brought down a pair of buildings there called the World Trade Center. Accepting the win, Bloomberg said, "New York is alive and well and open for business."

Mayors are elected by the people of their city or town. Mayors can be elected for **terms** of either two years or four years. In some cities, like Cincinnati, Ohio, the mayor can serve only a certain number of terms. In other cities, such as Boston, Massachusetts, there are no limits.

Before taking office, mayors are sworn in. They promise to uphold their communities' laws. Here, Mayor Ray Nagin, of New Orleans, Louisiana, is being sworn in.

Here, Washington, D.C., mayor Adrian Fenty (front left), city council members, and other city leaders speak out in favor of tighter laws on gun ownership in that city.

WORKING WITH THE CITY COUNCIL

Mayors do not run cities and towns by themselves. Most communities have a city council, made up of people who are also elected.

Some city councils hire a town manager to oversee the daily work of the city's different departments, such as the police, libraries, and parks.

The jobs of mayors and city councils are different in different places. In Los Angeles, mayors can name people to important jobs and offer a plan to spend the city's money. The city council then must allow or say no to the mayor's choices. In other cities, like Rock Hill, South Carolina, the mayor is part of the city council. The council works together to govern the town.

HOW WILL YOU PAY FOR IT?

In 2009, Philadelphia, Pennsylvania, mayor Michael Nutter needed money to keep libraries and swimming pools open. He asked the city council to increase taxes on many things people buy. The city council passed the plan. Paying police officers, buying slides for parks, and getting computers for libraries is expensive. Many mayors must come up with plans to bring in money for their town or city.

Cities and towns raise money in different ways. Many collect taxes based on the value of homes. Some charge for things like trash pickup and letting people park their cars in the street.

Cities and towns need money to pay for parks. Communities may have to buy land for new parks. Older parks often need new equipment, such as this green climber.

Here, Antonio Villaraigosa, the mayor of Los Angeles, talks to schoolchildren. Los Angeles is a very big city. It is home to more than 450,000 schoolchildren.

A BIG JOB
IN A BIG CITY

Millennium Park opened in Chicago, Illinois, in 2004. That day, Mayor Richard M. Daley was surrounded by artists, reporters, and powerful business people. "This park is **destined** to have a huge impact on this city," the mayor announced.

Some big cities have an official house in which the mayor can live. For example, New York's mayor calls Gracie Mansion home. In Los Angeles, the mayor lives at Getty House.

Mayors of big cities are on the job every day of the year. Thousands of people work for cities like New York, Chicago, and Los Angeles. These cities' schools educate hundreds of thousands of students. Their public train systems help millions of people get around each day. In big cities, daily newspapers and **bloggers** follow everything that the mayor does.

SMALL TOWN, NO SMALL TASK

Small-town mayors are not generally followed by news cameras. That does not make their jobs less important, though. These mayors make important decisions about things like hiring police officers or adding a stoplight to a busy road. They also work hard to bring new businesses to their towns.

On top of that, the mayors of small villages, townships, and **boroughs** often have other full-time jobs. For example, Mayor Christopher R. Seeley was still in high school when he was elected the mayor of Linesville, Pennsylvania, in 2005! Even though their time is limited, small-town mayors still take care of the people's needs.

Michael Sessions was just 18 years old when he was elected the mayor of Hillsdale, Michigan, in 2005. Several small towns, such as Hillsdale, have elected young mayors.

One fun thing that mayors get to do is walk in parades. Here, New York mayor Michael Bloomberg (second from left) walks in his city's St. Patrick's Day Parade.

RIBBON CUTTINGS AND PARADES

Washington, D.C., mayor Adrian Fenty **boasted** about his city's new playground on June 8, 2009. The park included swing sets and checkers tables. It also used **recycled** rubber mats. "We pride ourselves on putting the safety of our children first," he said.

A city's mayor is often the biggest cheerleader of the teams based there. For example, New York mayor Rudy Giuliani was often in the crowd when the New York Yankees played.

Being a mayor is not only hard work. Mayors often take part in ribbon-cutting **ceremonies** when new parks and buildings are opened. Mayors may be invited to throw out the first pitch at baseball games, too. They also judge **barbecue** contests at summer parties and lead holiday parades.

GREAT MAYORS OF THE PAST

Many mayors have left their mark on history. In 1926, Bertha Knight Landes, of Seattle, Washington, became the first woman to be elected mayor of a major American city. Norman Mineta became the first Asian-American mayor of a big city when San Jose, California, voters put him into office in 1971.

Tom Bradley was elected mayor of Los Angeles in 1973. He was the city's first African-American mayor. Bradley served as Los Angeles's mayor for 20 years. He even helped bring the **Olympic Games** to Los Angeles in 1984. Today, a part of the Los Angeles airport has been named after Bradley.

Los Angeles grew a lot during Tom Bradley's five terms as mayor. Bradley, seen here, worked hard to help the poor and to bring businesses to Los Angeles.

21

MAYORS OF TODAY AND TOMORROW

Today, mayors across the country are working to fix the problems in their communities. In Miami, Florida, Mayor Manuel Diaz took steps to build homes that families can afford. Portland, Maine, mayor Jill Duson is working to make the city's waterfront a place everyone can enjoy. In Pittsburgh, Pennsylvania, Mayor Luke Ravenstahl is hoping to make his city a center for **green building**.

All mayors need to hear from the people they serve. Take some time to learn about your local government. You could even get in touch with your mayor and offer your ideas on how to make your community a better place.

GLOSSARY

barbecue (BAHR-bih-kyoo) Having to do with a meal cooked outside on a grill or over an open fire.

bloggers (BLO-gerz) People who report their thoughts or findings on the Internet.

boasted (BOHST-ed) Talked with lots of pride.

boroughs (BUR-ohz) Towns or villages.

ceremonies (SER-ih-moh-neez) Special actions done on certain occasions.

destined (DES-tund) Meant for a purpose.

green building (GREEN BIL-ding) Building things in a way that does not hurt nature.

Olympic Games (uh-LIM-pik GAYMZ) When the best sports players in the world meet every four years to play against each other.

recycled (ree-SY-kuld) Made from something that could have been thrown away.

terms (TURMZ) Periods of time that an elected official can serve.

terrorists (TER-er-ists) People who use strong force to scare others.

tornadoes (tawr-NAY-dohz) Storms with funnel-shaped clouds that produce strong, spinning winds.

INDEX

WEB SITES

Due to the changing nature of Internet links, PowerKids Press has developed an online list of Web sites related to the subject of this book. This site is updated regularly. Please use this link to access the list:

www.powerkidslinks.com/hogw/mayor/